W9-ASY-367

CHILDREN'S *Living* FRENCH

PICTURE DICTIONARY

French-English English-French

by SUZANNE JACOB

Illustrations by BEA CURTIS

Crown Publishers, Inc., New York

ABOUT THIS DICTIONARY

The **Children's Living French Picture Dictionary** has been designed especially for younger children beginning to learn a new language. The Dictionary is meant to be used with the Children's Living French course. It contains a large proportion of the words as well as some phrases found in the recorded conversation.

The picture book format makes learning new words fun. Each picture is followed by both the French and the English word. Occasionally there are words without pictures—here the pictures would have been more confusing than helpful.

Most frequently words appear in the form used in the recorded conversation: singular or plural nouns, or infinitive or third person singular present tense verbs, as the case may be. Nouns are followed by the articles in parentheses while the feminine ending for adjectives is found in parentheses at the end of the words.

The **Children's Living French Picture Dictionary** can be used in various ways: to look up a word whose meaning is not clear; to play identification games; to serve as a model for drawing games as suggested by quizzes in the **Illustrated Manual;** and just as a fun book to look through. Each use will help build the child's French vocabulary.

Published by Living Language, a division of Crown Publishers, Inc., 225 Park Avenue South, New York, New York 10003.

LIVING LANGUAGE is a trademark and THE LIVING LANGUAGE COURSE is a Registered Trademark of Crown Publishers, Inc.

Manufactured in the United States of America

Library of Congress Catalog Card Number: 60-8615

ISBN 0-517-56332-0

1986 Updated Edition

10 9 8 7 6 5 4 3 2

A

à
    to, for

À bientôt!
    See you soon!

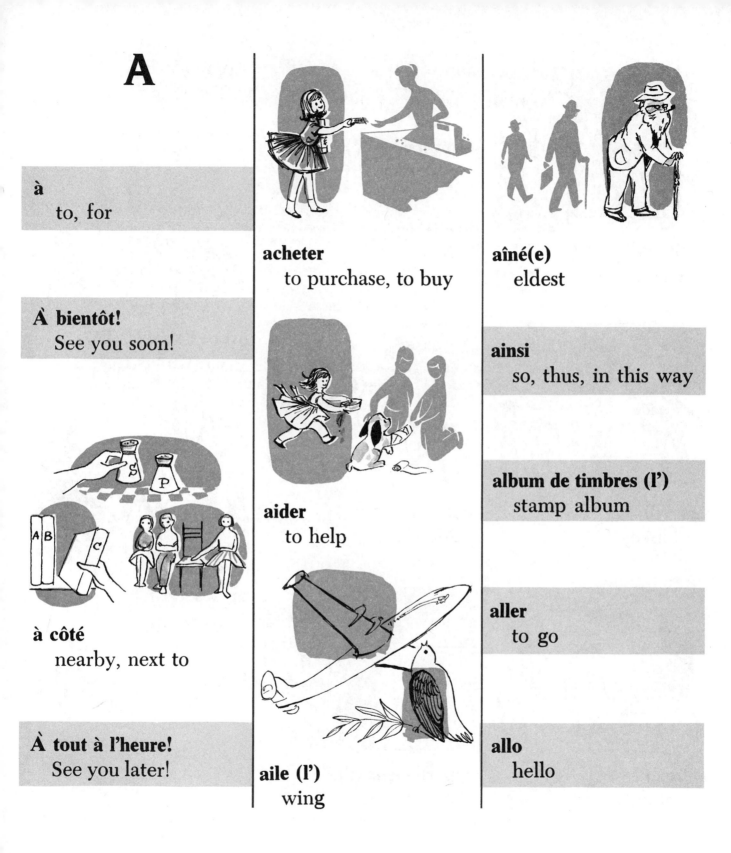

à côté
    nearby, next to

À tout à l'heure!
    See you later!

acheter
    to purchase, to buy

aider
    to help

aile (l')
    wing

aîné(e)
    eldest

ainsi
    so, thus, in this way

album de timbres (l')
    stamp album

aller
    to go

allo
    hello

3

ami(e) (l')
friend

année (l')
year

anniversaire (l')
birthday

ans (les)
years

Apprends-moi.
Teach me.

arbre de Noël (l')
Christmas tree

âne (l')
donkey

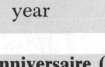

août
August

arbres (les)
trees

argent (l')
money, silver

animaux (les)
animals

appartement (l')
apartment

armoire (l')
closet, wardrobe

Assied!
Sit down!

assiette (l')
plate

Attends!
Wait!

au-dessus
above

au revoir
good-by

Au secours!
Help!

aussi
also

automne (l')
fall

autre
other

avec
with

avenue (l')
avenue

avion (l')
plane

avoir besoin de
to need

APRIL

avril
April

B

baiser
to kiss

balles (les)
balls

bas (les)
stockings

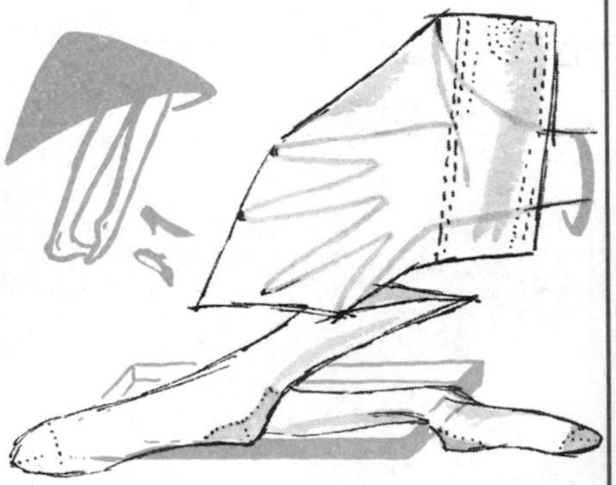

bas nylon (les)
nylon stockings

bateau (le)
boat

baton (le)
stick

beau (belle)
beautiful, pretty, nice

beaucoup
much, many

beurre (le)
butter

bien
well

billets (les)
tickets

blond(e)
blond

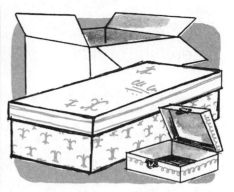

boite (la)
box

blanc(he)
white

blouse (la)
blouse, smock

Bon anniversaire!
Happy birthday!

boire
to drink

bleu(e)
blue

bois (le)
wood

bonbons (les)
candies

bonjour
good morning

Bonne Année!
Happy New Year!

bonnet (le)
cap

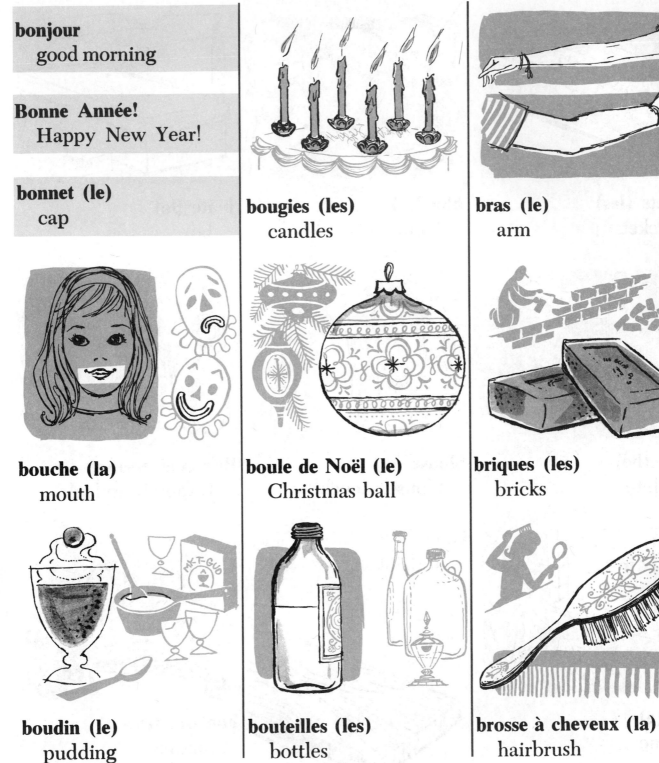

bougies (les)
candles

bras (le)
arm

bouche (la)
mouth

boule de Noël (le)
Christmas ball

briques (les)
bricks

boudin (le)
pudding

bouteilles (les)
bottles

brosse à cheveux (la)
hairbrush

brosse à dents (la)
toothbrush

bruit (le)
noise

brunette (la)
brunette

bûcheron (le)
woodcutter

buffet (le)
buffet, sideboard

bureau (le)
office, desk

C

cacahuètes (les)
peanuts

cacher
to hide

cadeau (le)
present, gift

café (le)
coffee, café

calendrier (le)
calendar

9

camarade de classe (le)
classmate

carte de Noël (la)
Christmas card

campagne (la)
country

canon (le)
cannon

cassé(e)
broken

cela
that

car
because

ceci
this

C'est difficile.
It's difficult (hard).

chacun(e)
each

chaises (les)
chairs

chambre à coucher (la)
bedroom

10

chambre (la)
room, bedroom

chameaux (les)
camels

chance (la)
luck

chanson (la)
song

chanter
to sing

chapeau (le)
hat

chat (le)
cat

chaud
warm, hot

chaudron (le)
caldron, pot

chaussures (les)
shoes

chaussures de bain
bathing slippers

cheminée (la)
chimney

11

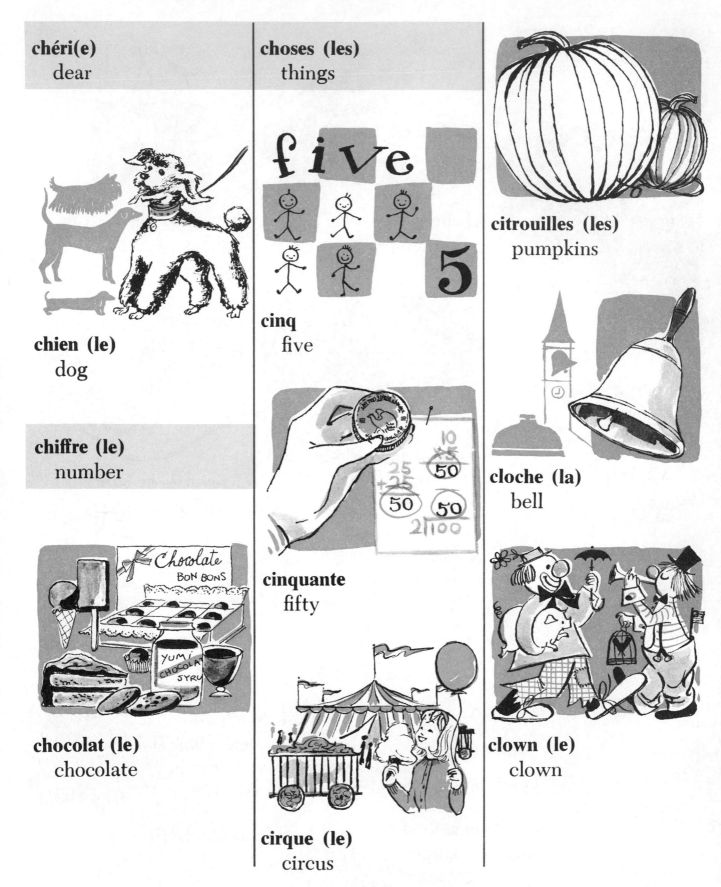

chéri(e)
dear

chien (le)
dog

chiffre (le)
number

chocolat (le)
chocolate

choses (les)
things

cinq
five

cinquante
fifty

cirque (le)
circus

citrouilles (les)
pumpkins

cloche (la)
bell

clown (le)
clown

12

cochons (les)
pigs

coeur (le)
heart

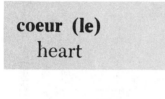

colonne (la)
column

combien
how many, how much

commencer
to start

Comment s'appelle-t-il?
What's his name?

Comment vas-tu?
How are you?

compter
to count

confiture (la)
jam, preserves

connaître
to know

construire
to build

coq (le)
rooster

couleurs (les)
colors

13

couper
  to cut

couvert(e)
  covered

crayon (le)
  pencil

courir
  to run

couvert (le)
  tableware

crayons de couleurs (les)
  colored pencils,
  crayons

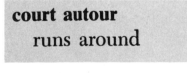

court autour
  runs around

craie (la)
  chalk

couteau (le)
  knife

crêpes (les)
  pancakes

14

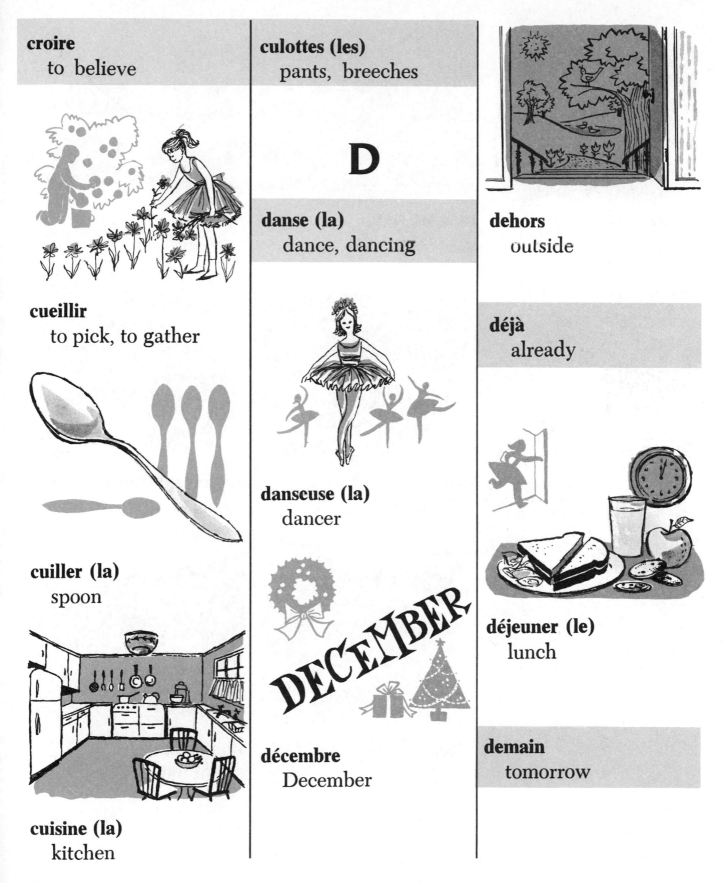

croire
to believe

cueillir
to pick, to gather

cuiller (la)
spoon

cuisine (la)
kitchen

culottes (les)
pants, breeches

D

danse (la)
dance, dancing

danscuse (la)
dancer

décembre
December

dehors
outside

déjà
already

déjeuner (le)
lunch

demain
tomorrow

15

demande (la)
question

demande
requests, asks

dent (la)
tooth

dents (les)
teeth

Dépêche-toi!
Hurry up!

dessert (le)
dessert

dessiner
to draw

deux
two

devant
before, in front of

devanture (la)
store window

dimanche
Sunday

16

dire
to say

dix
ten

dix-huit
eighteen

dix-neuf
nineteen

dix-sept
seventeen

docteur (le)
doctor

doigt (le)
finger

dormir
to sleep

douze
twelve

douleur (la)
pain

17

E

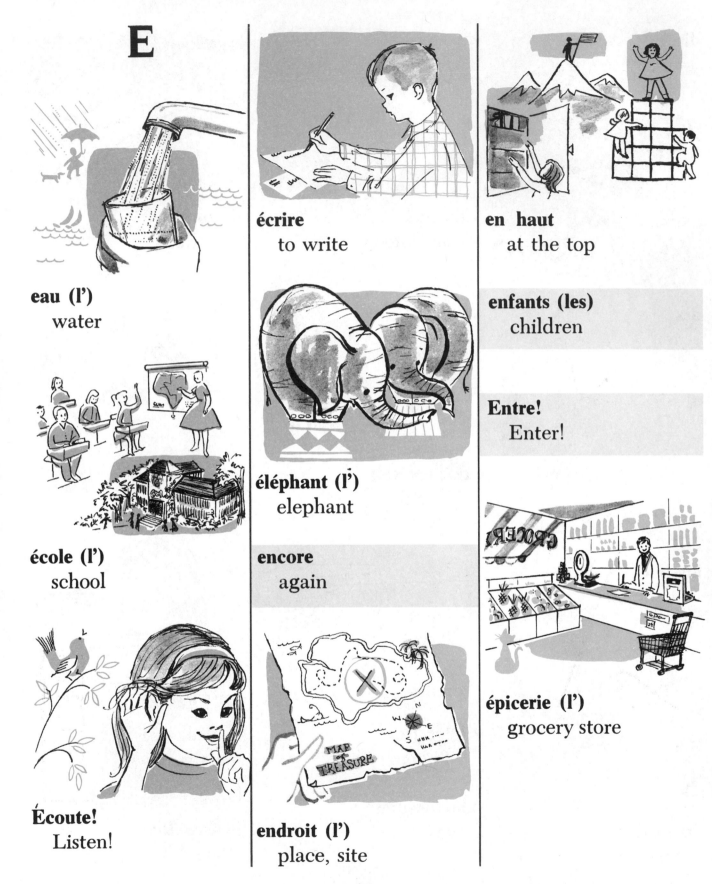

eau (l')
water

école (l')
school

Écoute!
Listen!

écrire
to write

éléphant (l')
elephant

encore
again

endroit (l')
place, site

en haut
at the top

enfants (les)
children

Entre!
Enter!

épicerie (l')
grocery store

estomac (l')
stomach

été (l')
summer

étoile (l')
star

F

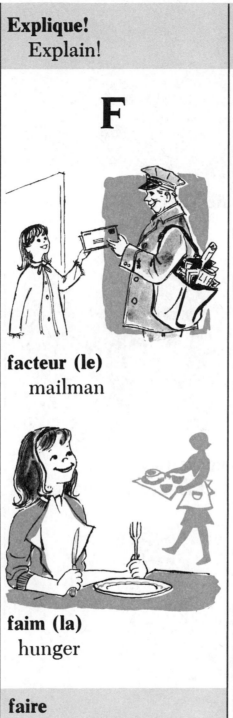

facteur (le)
mailman

faim (la)
hunger

faire
to do, make

famille (la)
family

fatigué(e)
tired

femme (la)
woman

fenêtre (la)
window

ferme (la)
farm

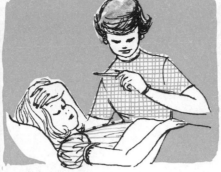

fièvre (la)
fever

film (le)
movie, film

feuille (la)
leaf

figure (la)
face, form, shape

fils (le)
son

février
February

fille (la)
girl, daughter

fleurs (les)
flowers

flûte (la)
flute

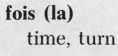

fois (la)
time, turn

forêt (la)
forest

foulard (le)
scarf

fourchette (la)
fork

fourneau (le)
stove

français
French

fraise (la)
strawberry

frapper
to knock

frère (le)
brother

fruits (les)
fruits

G

gamin (le), gamine (la)
youngster

21

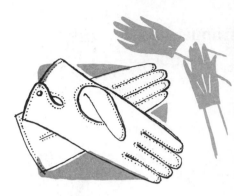

gants (les)
gloves

garçons (les)
boys

gâteau (le)
cake

gâteau d'anniversaire (le)
birthday cake

gentilhomme (le)
gentleman

glace (la)
ice cream

goûter d'anniversaire (le)
birthday party

grand(e)
tall

grand-mère (la)
grandmother

grand-père (le)
grandfather

grimpe
climbs

grosse femme (la)
fat lady

H

habiller
to dress

habitent
live in (they)

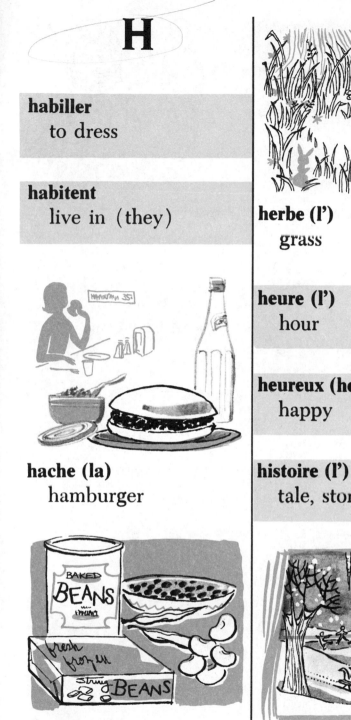

hache (la)
hamburger

haricots (les)
beans

herbe (l')
grass

heure (l')
hour

heureux (heureuse)
happy

histoire (l')
tale, story

hiver (l')
winter

homme (l')
man

horloge (l')
clock

huile (l')
oil

huit
 eight

I

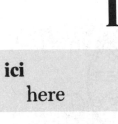

ici
 here

il
 he, it

Il est deux heures.
 It is two o'clock.

Il est six heures trente.
 It is six-thirty.

Il est une heure.
 It is one o'clock.

Il fait chaud.
 It is warm.

Il fait froid.
 It is cold.

Il n'y a pas le temps.
 There isn't time.

il y avait
 there were

J

jamais
 never

janvier
January

jardin (le)
garden

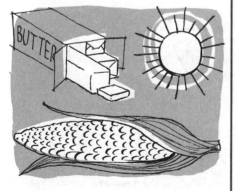

jaune
yellow

je
I

J'ai peur.
I'm afraid.

Je me lève.
I get up.

Je ne sais pas.
I don't know.

Je sais.
I know.

Je suis malade.
I am sick.

jeu (le)
game

jeudi
Thursday

joli(e)
pretty

jouer
to play

jouer à cache-cache
to play hide and seek

jour (le)
day

Joyeux Noël!
Merry Christmas!

juillet
July

juin
June

jupe (la)
skirt

jus (le)
juice

jus d'orange (le)
orange juice

L

lac (le)
lake

laine (la)
wool

lait (le)
milk

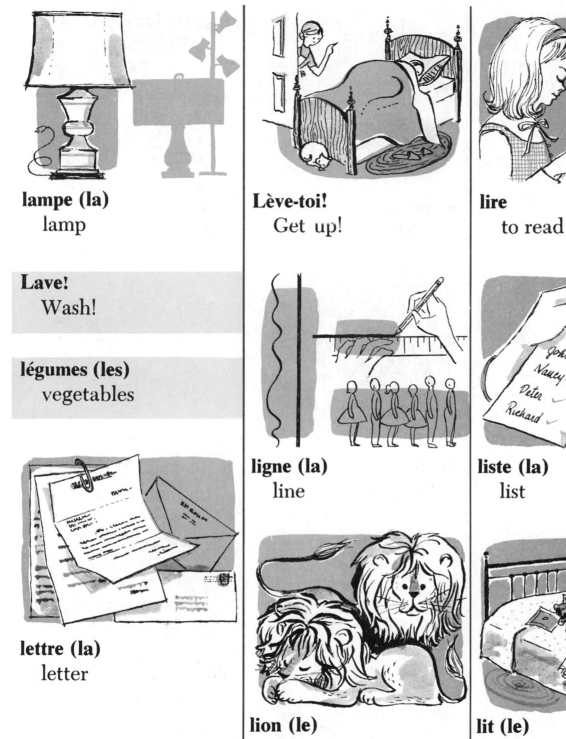

lampe (la)
lamp

Lève-toi!
Get up!

lire
to read

Lave!
Wash!

légumes (les)
vegetables

ligne (la)
line

liste (la)
list

lettre (la)
letter

lion (le)
lion

lit (le)
bed

livres (les)
pounds

lumières (les)
lights

mai
May

livre (le)
book

lundi
Monday

maillots de bain (les)
bathing suits

livre d'image (le)
picture book

M

main (la)
hand

loup (le)
wolf

magasin (le)
store

maintenant
now

mais
but

mal à la tete
headache

Manges!
Eat!

maison (la)
house

mal aux dents
toothache

manteau (le)
coat

malade
sick

mal à la gorge
sore throat

maman (la)
mama

**marchand (le),
marchande (la)**
storekeeper

marchent
walk (they)

mardi
Tuesday

mari (le)
husband

marionnettes (les)
puppets

MARCH

mars
March

matin (le)
morning

méchant(e)
wicked, evil

médicament (le)
medicine

mer (la)
sea

merci
thanks

mercredi
Wednesday

mère (la)
mother

30

met
puts

mettre
to put on

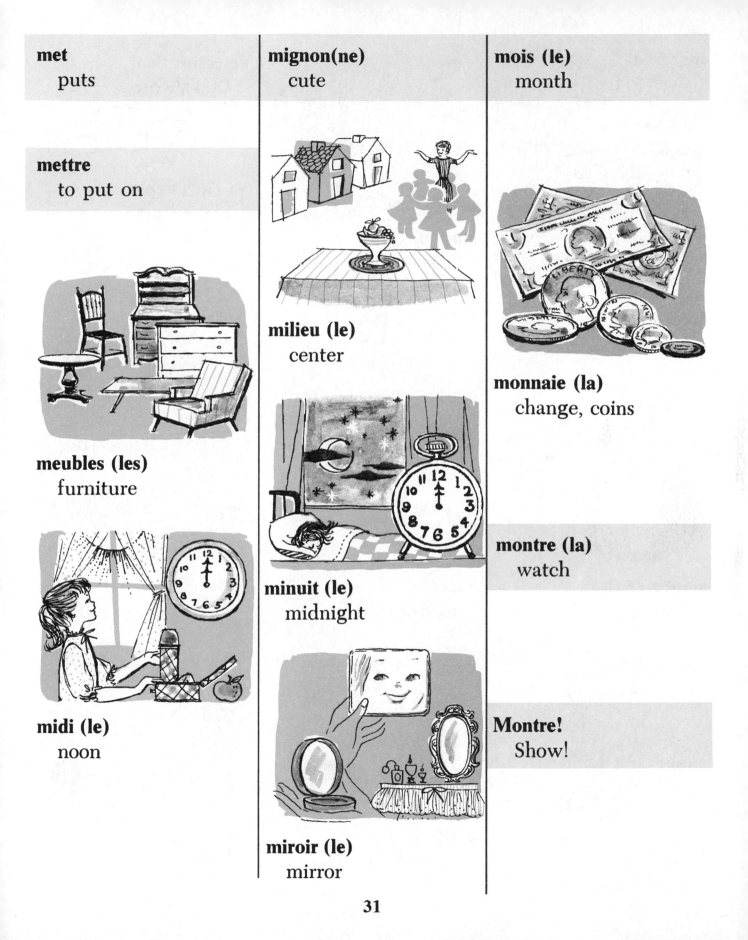

meubles (les)
furniture

midi (le)
noon

mignon(ne)
cute

milieu (le)
center

minuit (le)
midnight

miroir (le)
mirror

mois (le)
month

monnaie (la)
change, coins

montre (la)
watch

Montre!
Show!

31

morceaux (les)
pieces

mot (le)
word

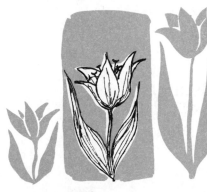

mouchoir (le)
handkerchief

moyen(ne)
medium,
medium-sized

musique (la)
music

N

nager
to swim

nappe (la)
tablecloth

Ne crains rien.
Don't worry.

Ne t'arrête pas.
Don't stop.

neige (la)
snow

neuf
nine

32

nez (le)
nose

Noël
Christmas

noir(e)
black

nombre (le)
number

N'oubliez pas.
Don't forget.

nous avons
we have

nouveau (nouvelle)
new

novembre
November

O

octobre
October

oeufs (les)
eggs

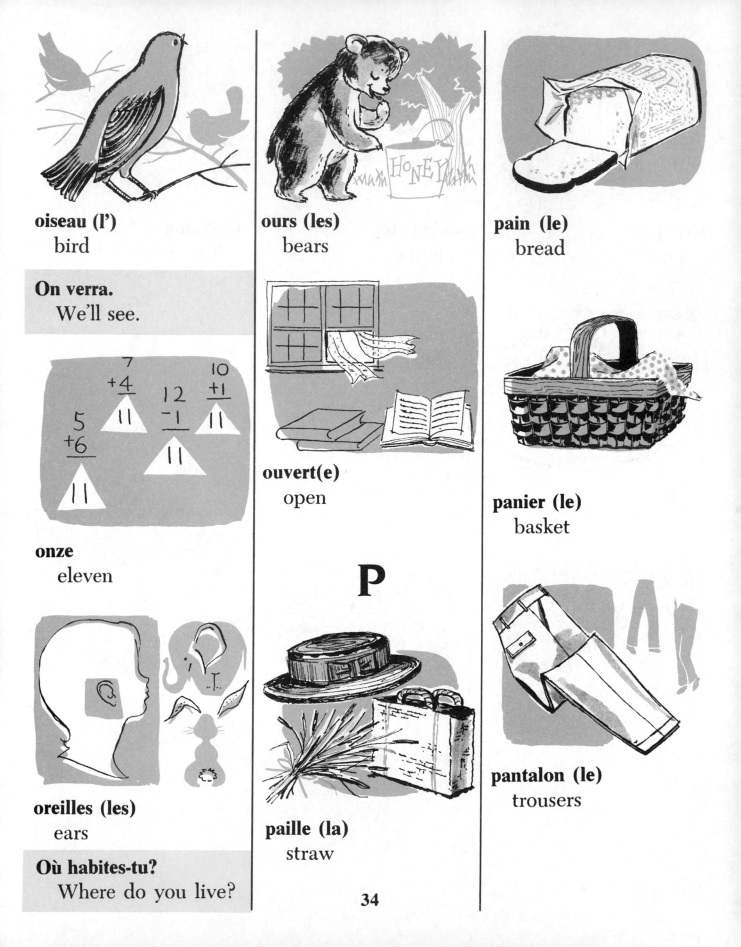

oiseau (l')
bird

On verra.
We'll see.

onze
eleven

oreilles (les)
ears

Où habites-tu?
Where do you live?

ours (les)
bears

ouvert(e)
open

P

paille (la)
straw

pain (le)
bread

panier (le)
basket

pantalon (le)
trousers

34

papier (le)
paper

parents (les)
parents

paresseux
lazy

paquet (le)
package, parcel

par ici
this way

parler
to talk, to speak

par terre
on the floor

partout
everywhere

parce que
because

parade (la)
parade

pardessus (le)
overcoat

patin (les)
ice skates

pâtisserie (la)
bakery

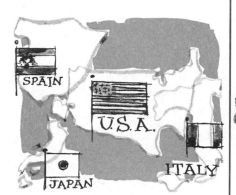

pays (les)
countries

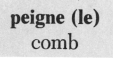

peigne (le)
comb

pelle (la)
shovel

penser
to think

perdu(e)
lost

père (le)
father

petit(e)
small

Petit Chaperon Rouge
Little Red Riding
Hood

petite chose (la)
snack

petit déjeuner (le)
breakfast

petits gâteaux (les)
cookies

pistolets (les)
pistols

plancher (le)
floor

piano (le)
piano

plafond (le)
ceiling

plat (le)
dish

pied (le)
foot

plage (la)
beach

pleurer
to cry, to weep

plaire
to please

plissé(e)
pleated

plume (la)
pen

poésie (la)
poem, poetry

poil (le)
hair, fur

poisson (le)
fish

poivrière (la)
pepper shaker

pomme (la)
apple

pommes de terre (les)
potatoes

porte (la)
door

porter
to bear, to carry,
to wear

poule (la)
hen

poulet (le)
chicken

poupée (la)
doll

38

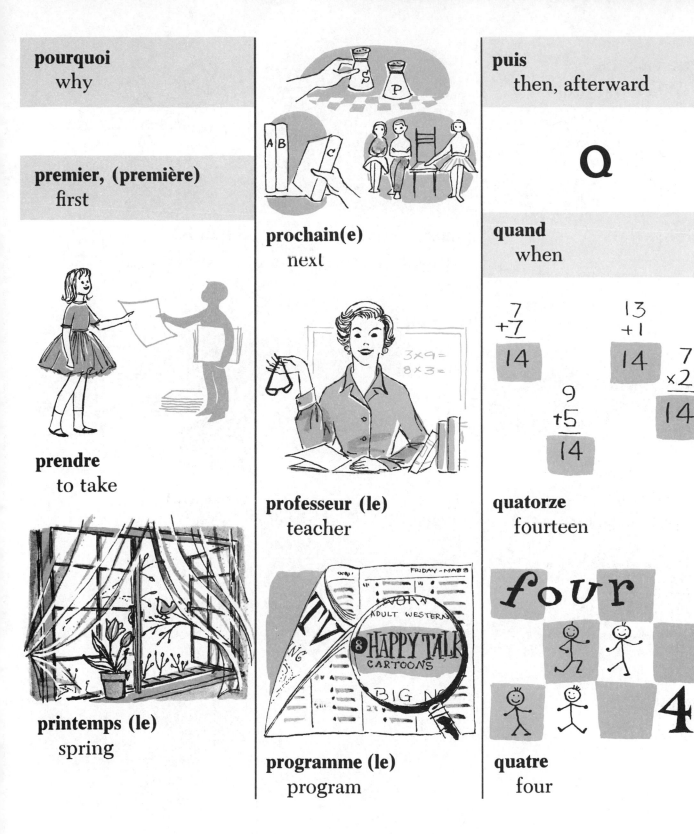

pourquoi
why

premier, (première)
first

prendre
to take

printemps (le)
spring

prochain(e)
next

professeur (le)
teacher

programme (le)
program

puis
then, afterward

Q

quand
when

$$\begin{array}{r} 7 \\ +7 \\ \hline 14 \end{array}$$

$$\begin{array}{r} 13 \\ +1 \\ \hline 14 \end{array}$$

$$\begin{array}{r} 7 \\ \times 2 \\ \hline 14 \end{array}$$

$$\begin{array}{r} 9 \\ +5 \\ \hline 14 \end{array}$$

quatorze
fourteen

four

quatre
four

Que veux-tu?
What do you want?

quel(le)
which, what

Quel âge as-tu?
How old are you?

Quelle heure est-il?
What time is it?

queue (la)
tail

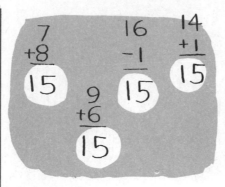

quinze
fifteen

Qu'y a-t-il?
What is it?

R

raisins (les)
grapes

Regarde!
Look!

repas (le)
meal

Répète!
Repeat!

réponse (la)
answer

Reste au lit!
Stay in bed!

Trois Rois Mages (les)
Three Wise Men

route (la)
road

réveiller
to awaken

rosbif (le)
roast beef

ruban (le)
ribbon, band

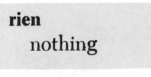

rien
nothing

rouge
red

rue (la)
street

robe (la)
dress, gown

41

S

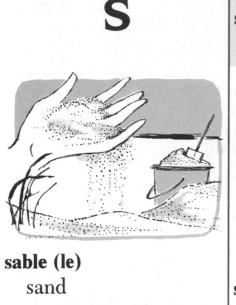

sable (le)
sand

sac (le)
bag

Saint Nicolas
Santa Claus

salière (la)
saltcellar

salle à manger (la)
dining room

salle de bain (la)
bathroom

salon (le)
living room

samedi
Saturday

sandwich (le)
sandwich

42

s'appeler
to be named

saveur (la)
flavor

saute
jumps

se moquent de
laugh at, make fun of (they)

savon (le)
soap

se promener
to take a walk

se couche
lies down

se rappeler
to remember, to recall

seize
sixteen

semaine (la)
week

s'endort
sleeps (goes to sleep)

sept
seven

septembre
September

six
six

serviette (la)
napkin, towel

silence (le)
silence

s'il te plaît
please

soeur (la)
sister

soir (le)
evening

singes (les)
monkeys

siège (le)
seat

sirop (le)
syrup

soleil (le)
sun

sommeil (le)
sleep, sleepiness

sorte (la)
kind, manner, way

sortir
to go out

sot(te)
silly

soudain(e)
sudden

soufflerai
huff (I'll)

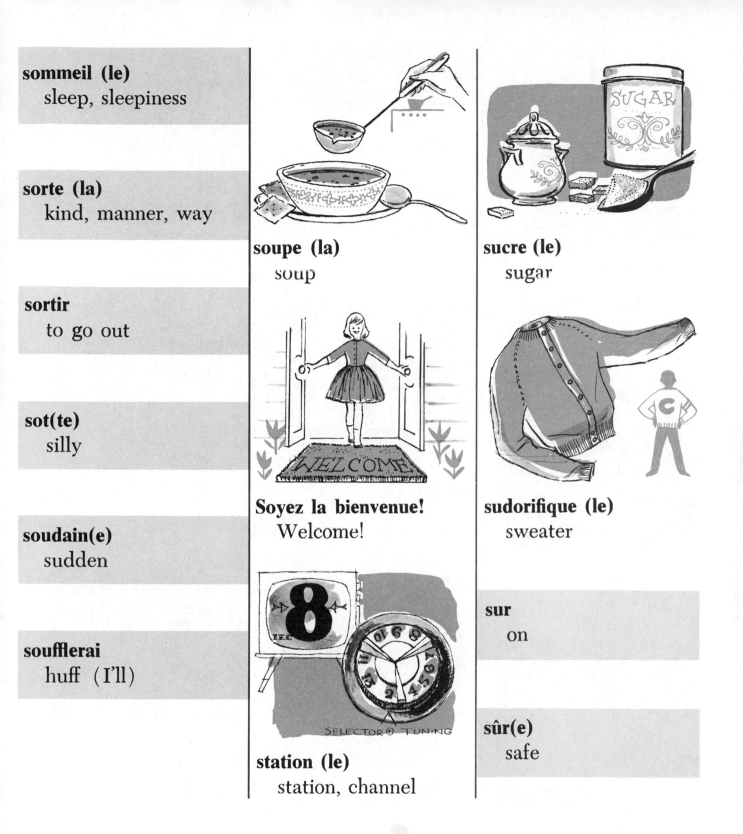

soupe (la)
soup

Soyez la bienvenue!
Welcome!

station (le)
station, channel

sucre (le)
sugar

sudorifique (le)
sweater

sur
on

sûr(e)
safe

45

T

table (la)
table

tableau noir (le)
blackboard

tablier (le)
apron

tard
late

tasse (la)
cup

taureau (le)
bull

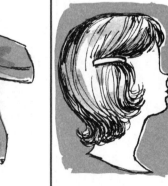

téléphone (le)
telephone

télévision (la)
television

tellement
so much

temps (le)
time, weather

tête (la)
head

toit (le)
roof

tomber
to fall

tôt
early, soon

toucher
to touch

tout(e)
all

train (le)
train

travailler
to work

traverser
to cross

treize
thirteen

trente
thirty

très
very

trois
three

47

tu
you

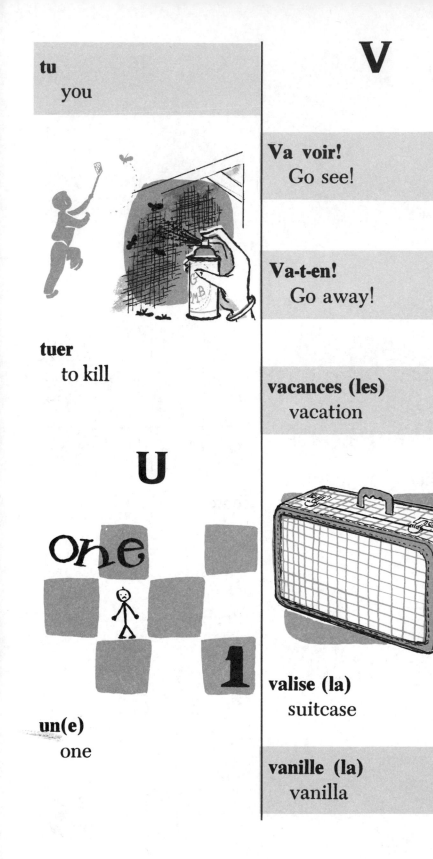

tuer
to kill

U

un(e)
one

V

Va voir!
Go see!

Va-t-en!
Go away!

vacances (les)
vacation

valise (la)
suitcase

vanille (la)
vanilla

vendredi
Friday

verre (le)
glass, water glass

vert(e)
green

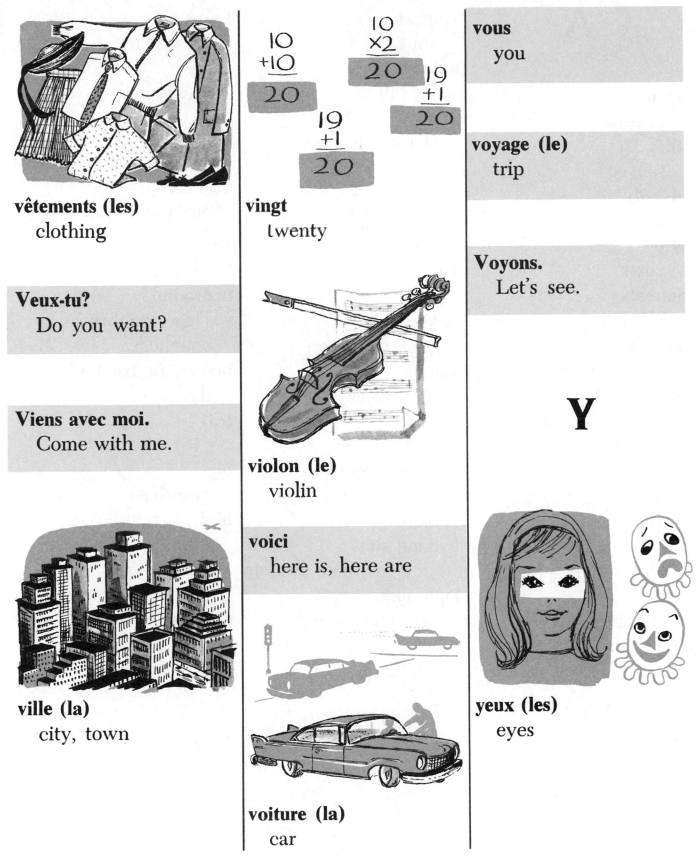

vêtements (les)
clothing

Veux-tu?
Do you want?

Viens avec moi.
Come with me.

ville (la)
city, town

10
+10
20

10
×2
20

19
+1
20

19
+1
20

vingt
twenty

violon (le)
violin

voici
here is, here are

voiture (la)
car

vous
you

voyage (le)
trip

Voyons.
Let's see.

Y

yeux (les)
eyes

49

A

again
encore
all
tout(e)
already
déjà
also
aussi
animals
(les) animaux
answer
(la) réponse
apartment
(l') appartement
apple
(la) pomme
April
avril
apron
(le) tablier
arm
(le) bras
at the top
en haut

August
août
autumn
see fall
avenue
(l') avenue

B

bag
(le) sac
bakery
(la) pâtisserie
balls
(les) balles
basket
(le) panier
bathing slippers
(les) chaussures de
bain
bathing suits
(les) maillots de bain
bathroom
(la) salle de bain
beach
(la) plage

beans
(les) haricots
bears
(les) ours
beautiful, pretty, nice
beau (belle)
because
car, parce que
bed
(le) lit
bedroom
(la) chambre à
coucher
before, in front of
devant
bell
(la) cloche
big
grand(e)
bird
(l') oiseau
birthday
(l') anniversaire
birthday cake
(le) gâteau
d'anniversaire

birthday party
(le) goûter
d'anniversaire

black
noir(e)

blackboard
(le) tableau noir

blond
blond(e)

blouse, smock
(la) blouse

blue
bleu(e)

boat
(le) bateau

book
(le) livre

bottles
(les) bouteilles

box
(la) boîte

boys
(les) garçons

bread
(le) pain

breakfast
(le) petit déjeuner

bricks
(les) briques

broken
cassé(e)

brother
(le) frère

brunette
(la) brunette

buffet, sideboard
(le) buffet

bull
(le) taureau

but
mais

butter
(le) beurre

C

cake
(le) gâteau

caldron, pot
(le) chaudron

calendar
(le) calendrier

camels
(les) chameaux

candies
(les) bonbons

candles
(les) bougies

cannon
(le) canon

cap
(le) bonnet

car
(la) voiture

cat
(le) chat

ceiling
(le) plafond

center
(le) milieu

chairs
(les) chaises

chalk
(la) craie

change, coins
(la) monnaie

channel
see station

chicken
 (le) poulet
children
 (les) enfants
chimney
 (la) cheminée
chocolate
 (le) chocolat
Christmas
 Noël
Christmas ball
 (le) boule de Noël
Christmas card
 (la) carte de Noël
Christmas tree
 (l')arbre de Noël
circus
 (le) cirque
city, town
 (la) ville
classmate
 (le) camarade de classe
climbs
 grimpe
clock
 (l')horloge
closet, wardrobe
 (l')armoire

clothing
 (les) vêtements
clown
 (le) clown
coat
 (le) manteau
coffee, café
 (le) café
colored pencils, crayons
 (les) crayons de couleurs
colors
 (les) couleurs
column
 (la) colonne
comb
 (le) peigne
Come with me.
 Viens avec moi.
cookies
 (les) petits gâteaux
countries
 (les) pays
country
 (la) campagne
covered
 couvert(e)
cup
 (la) tasse

cute
 mignon(ne)

D

dance
 (la) danse
dancer
 (la) danseuse
day
 (le) jour
dear
 chéri(e)
December
 décembre
dessert
 (le) dessert
dining room
 (la) salle à manger
dish
 (le) plat
Do you want?
 Veux-tu?
doctor
 (le) docteur
dog
 (le) chien

doll
(la) poupée
donkey
(l') âne
Don't forget.
N'oubliez pas.
Don't stop.
Ne t'arrête pas.
Don't worry.
Ne crains rien.
door
(la) porte
dress, gown
(la) robe

E

each
chacun(e)
early, soon
tôt
ears
(les) oreilles
Eat!
Manges!
eggs
(les) oeufs

eight
huit
eighteen
dix-huit
eldest
aîné(e)
elephant
(l') éléphant
cleven
onze
Enter!
Entre!
evening
(le) soir
everyone
tout le monde
everywhere
partout
Explain!
Explique!
eyes
(les) yeux

F

face, form, shape
(la) figure

fall
(l') automne
family
(la) famille
farm
(la) ferme
fat lady
(la) grosse femme
father
(le) père
February
février
fever
(la) fièvre
fifteen
quinze
fifty
cinquante
finger
(le) doigt
first
premier (première)
fish
(le) poisson
five
cinq
flavor
(la) saveur

floor
(le) plancher
flowers
(les) fleurs
flute
(la) flûte
foot
(le) pied
forest
(la) forêt
fork
(la) fourchette
forty
quarante
four
quatre
fourteen
quatorze
French
français
Friday
vendredi
friends
(les) ami(e)s
fruits
(les) fruits
fruit salad
(la) salade de fruits
furniture
(les) meubles

G

game
(le) jeu
garden
(le) jardin
gentleman
(le) gentilhomme
Get up!
Lève-toi!
girl
(la) fille
give me
donnez-moi
glass, water glass
(le) verre
gloves
(les) gants
Go away!
Va-t-en!
Go see!
Va voir!
good-by
au revoir
good morning
bonjour
grandfather
(le) grandpère

grandmother
(la) grandmère
grapes
(les) raisins
grass
(l') herbe
green
vert(e)
grocery store
(l') épicerie

H

hair, fur
(le) poil
hairbrush
(la) brosse à cheveux
hamburger
(la) hache
hand
(la) main
handkerchief
(le) mouchoir
happy
heureux (heureuse)
Happy birthday!
Bon anniversaire!
Happy New Year!
Bonne Année!

hat
(le) chapeau
head
(la) tête
headache
mal à la tête
heart
(le) coeur
he, it
il
hello
allo
Help!
Au secours!
hen
(la) poule
here
ici
here is, here are
voici
hour
(l') heure
house
(la) maison
How are you?
Comment vas-tu?
how many, how much
combien
How old are you?
Quel âge as-tu?

huff (I'll)
soufflerai
hunger
(la) faim
Hurry up!
Dépêche-toi!
husband
(le) mari

I

I
je
I'm afraid.
J'ai peur.
I am sick.
Je suis malade.
I don't know.
Je ne sais pas.
I get up.
Je me lève.
I know.
Je sais.
ice cream
(la) glace
ice skates
(les) patins
It is cold.
Il fait froid.

It's difficult (hard).
C'est difficile.
It is one o'clock.
Il est une heure.
It is six-thirty.
Il est six heures trente.
It is two o'clock.
Il est deux heures.
It is warm.
Il fait chaud.

J

jam, preserves
(la) confiture
January
janvier
juice
(le) jus
July
juillet
jumps
saute
June
juin

K

kind, manner, way
(la) sorte

kitchen
   (la) cuisine
knife
   (le) couteau

L

lake
   (le) lac
lamp
   (la) lampe
late
   tard
laugh at, make fun of (they)
   se moquent de
lazy
   paresseux
leaf
   (la) feuille
Let's see.
   Voyons.
letter
   (la) lettre
lies down
   se couche
lights
   (les) lumières

line
   (la) ligne
lion
   (le) lion
list
   (la) liste
Listen!
   Écoute!
little, small
   petit(e)
Little Red Riding Hood
   Petit Chaperon Rouge
live in (they)
   habitent
living room
   (le) salon
Look!
   Regarde!
lost
   perdu(e)
luck
   (la) chance
lunch
   (le) déjeuner

M

mailman
   (le) facteur

man
   (l')homme
March
   mars
May
   mai
meal
   (le) repas
medicine
   (le) médicament
medium, medium-sized
   moyen(ne)

Merry Christmas!
   Joyeux Noël!

midday
   see noon
midnight
   (le) minuit
milk
   (le) lait
mirror
   (le) miroir
Monday
   lundi
money, silver
   (l') argent
monkeys
   (les) singes

month
  (le) mois
morning
  (le) matin
mother
  (la) mère
mama
  (la) maman
mouth
  (la) bouche
movie, film
  (le) film
much, many
  beaucoup
music
  (la) musique

N

napkin, towel
  (la) serviette
nearby, next to
  à côté
never
  jamais
new
  nouveau (nouvelle)
next
  prochain(e)

nine
  neuf
nineteen
  dix-neuf
noise
  (le) bruit
noon
  (le) midi
nose
  (le) nez
nothing
  rien
November
  novembre
now
  maintenant
number
  (le) nombre
  (le) chiffre
nylon stockings
  (les) bas nylon

O

October
  octobre
office, desk
  (le) bureau

oil
  (l') huile
on
  sur
on the floor
  par terre
one
  un(e)
open
  ouvert(e)
orange juice
  (le) jus d'orange
other
  autre
outside
  dehors
overcoat
  (le) pardessus

P

package, parcel
  (le) paquet
pain
  (la) douleur
pancakes
  (les) crêpes

pants, breeches
(les) culottes

paper
(le) papier

parade
(la) parade

parents
(les) parents

peanuts
(les) cacahuètes

pen
(la) plume

pencil
(le) crayon

pepper shaker
(la) poivrière

piano
(le) piano

picture book
(le) livre d'images

pieces
(les) morceaux

pigs
(les) cochons

pistols
(les) pistolets

place, site
(l') endroit

plane
(l') avion

plate
(l') assiette

please
s'il te plaît

pleated
plissé(e)

poem, poetry
(la) poésie

pot
see caldron

potatoes
(les) pommes de terre

pounds
(les) livres

present, gift
cadeau (le)

pretty
joli(e)

program
(le) programme

pudding
(le) boudin

pumpkins
(les) citrouilles

puppets
(les) marionnettes

puts
met

Q

question
(la) demande

R

red
rouge

Repeat!
Répète!

requests, asks
demande

ribbon, band
(le) ruban

road
(la) route

roast beef
(le) rosbif

roof
(le) toit

room, bedroom
(la) chambre

rooster
(le) coq
runs around
court autour

S

safe
sûr(e)
saltcellar
(la) salière
sand
(le) sable
sandwich
(le) sandwich
Santa Claus
Saint Nicolas
Saturday
samedi
scarf
(le) foulard
school
(l') école
sea
(la) mer

seat
(le) siège
See you later!
À tout à l'heure!
See you soon!
À bientôt!
September
septembre
seven
sept
seventeen
dix-sept
shoes
(les) chaussures
shovels
(les) pelles
Show!
Montre!
sick
malade
silence
(le) silence
silly
sot(te)
sister
(la) soeur

Sit down!
Assied!
six
six
sixteen
seize
skirt
(la) jupe
sleep, sleepiness
(le) sommeil
sleeps (goes to sleep)
s'endort
small
petit(e)
snack
(la) petite chose
snow
(la) neige
so, thus, in this way
ainsi
so much
tellement
soap
(le) savon
son
(le) fils
song
(la) chanson

sore throat
mal à la gorge
soup
(la) soupe
spoon
(la) cuiller
spring
(le) printemps
stamp album
(l') album de timbres
star
(l') étoile
station, channel
(la) station
Stay in bed!
Reste au lit!
stick
(le) baton
stockings
(les) bas
stomach
(l') estomac
store
(le) magasin
storekeeper
(le) marchand,
(la) marchande

store window
(la) devanture
stove
(le) fourneau
straw
(la) paille
strawberry
(la) fraise
street
(la) rue
sudden
soudain(e)
sugar
(le) sucre
suitcase
(la) valise
summer
(l') été
sun
(le) soleil
Sunday
dimanche
sweater
(le) sudorifique
syrup
(le) sirop

T

table
(la) table
tablecloth
(la) nappe
tableware
(le) couvert
tail
(la) queue
tale, story
(l') histoire
tall
grand(e)
Teach me.
Apprends-moi.
teacher
(le) professeur
teeth
(les) dents
telephone
(le) téléphone
television
(la) télévision

ten
dix

thanks
merci

that
cela

then, afterward
puis

There isn't time.
Il n'y a pas le temps.

there were
il y avait

things
(les) choses

thirteen
treize

thirty
trente

this
ceci

this way
par ici

three
trois

Three Wise Men
(les) Trois Rois Mages

Thursday
jeudi

tickets
(les) billets

time, weather
(le) temps

time, turn
(la) fois

tired
fatigué(e)

to, for
à

to awaken
réveiller

to be named
s'appeler

to bear, to carry, to wear
porter

to believe
croire

to build
construire

to count
compter

to cross
traverser

to cry, to weep
pleurer

to cut
couper

to do, to make
faire

to draw
dessiner

to dress
habiller

to drink
boire

to fall
tomber

to go
aller

to go out
sortir

to help
aider

to hide
cacher

to kill
tuer

to kiss
baiser

to knock frapper	**to sleep** dormir	**towel** (la) serviette
to know connaître	**to start** commencer	**train** (le) train
to need avoir besoin de	**to swim** nager	**trees** (les) arbres
to pick, to gather cueillir	**to take** prendre	**trip** (le) voyage
to play jouer	**to take a walk** se promener	**trousers** (le) pantalon
to play hide and seek jouer à cache-cache	**to talk, to speak** parler	**Tuesday** mardi
to please plaire	**to think** penser	**twelve** douze
to purchase, to buy acheter	**to touch** toucher	**twenty** vingt
to put on mettre	**to work** travailler	**two** deux
to read lire	**to write** écrire	
to remember, to recall se rappeler	**tomorrow** demain	
to run courir	**tooth** (la) dent	
to say dire	**toothache** mal aux dents	# U
to sing chanter	**toothbrush** (la) brosse à dents	**until, till** jusqu'à, jusqu'à ce que

V

vacation
(les) vacances
vanilla
(la) vanille
vegetables
(les) légumes
very
très
violin
(le) violon

W

Wait!
Attends!
walk (they)
marchant
warm, hot
chaud
Wash!
Lave!
watch
(la) montre

water
(l') eau
we have
nous avons
We'll see.
On verra.
Wednesday
mercredi
week
(la) semaine
Welcome!
Soyez la bienvenue!
well
bien
What do you want?
Que veux-tu?
What's his name?
Comment s'appelle-t-il?
What is it?
Qu'est-ce que c'est?
Qu'y a-t-il?
What time is it?
Quelle heure est-il?
when
quand
Where do you live?
Où habites-tu?

which, what
quel(le)
white
blanc(he)
why
pourquoi
wicked, evil
méchant(e)
window
(la) fenêtre
wing
(l') aile
winter
(l') hiver
with
avec
wolf
(le) loup
woman
(la) femme
woodcutter
(le) bûcheron
wood
(le) bois
wool
(la) laine
word
(le) mot

Y

year
(l') année

years
(les) ans

yellow
jaune

you
tu, vous

youngster
(le) gamin,
(la) gamine